Why Do We Have to Go to School?

School poems
collected by John Foster

OXFORD
UNIVERSITY PRESS

OXFORD
UNIVERSITY PRESS

Great Clarendon Street, Oxford OX2 6DP

Oxford University Press is a department of the University of Oxford.
It furthers the University's objective of excellence in research, scholarship,
and education by publishing worldwide in

Oxford New York

Auckland Bangkok Buenos Aires
Cape Town Chennai Dar es Salaam Delhi Hong Kong Istanbul
Karachi Kolkata Kuala Lumpur Madrid Melbourne Mexico City Mumbai
Nairobi São Paulo Shanghai Singapore Taipei Tokyo Toronto
with an associated company in Berlin

Oxford is a registered trade mark of Oxford University Press
in the UK and in certain other countries

British Library Cataloguing in Publication Data available

ISBN 0-19-276282-6

1   3   5   7   9   10   8   6   4   2

Typeset by Mary Tudge (Typesetting Services)

Printed in the UK by Cox & Wyman Ltd, Reading, Berkshire

Cover and inside illustrations by Ellis Nadler

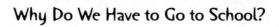

Why Do We Have to Go to School?

Contents

Sing a Song of Schooltime

Sing a song of schooltime,
A pocket full of play
Four and twenty children
Working through the day,

When the class was over,
The kids began to sing,
Time for fun and a bucket of sun
Until the bell shall ring.

The kids are in the playground,
Where it's nice and sunny,
Teacher's in the staffroom
Eating bread and honey,
The head is in the office,
Twiddling her toes,
When in came a naughty boy,
Picking at his nose!

Andrew Fusek Peters

Late Again

Off to school,
I'm late again,
hurrying, scurrying
down the lane
past the oak tree,
past the gate
where the white cat
sits and waits,
past the postman,
past old Mabel
putting bird seed
on a table,
past Mr Bates
who's pruning roses,
past his fat black
spaniel, Moses
to where the crossing
lady stands
lollipop
clutched in her hands.
All the traffic
has to wait.
It toots, it hoots,
'You're late! You're late!'

Marian Swinger

Cross-Boss

Lollipop lady
takes some licking,
spends her time in
tick-tick-ticking
off us kids,
gives too much stick—in fact, of her, we're really
sick—in-
deed
we
need
a
sweeter
sort—
not
a
bossy,
cross
escort.

Gina Douthwaite

How Alarming

On the front door of our school
There is a notice which says:
     WARNING
This school is alarmed.

'I'm not surprised,' says Dad.
'The way you lot behave,
I'd be alarmed
If I was responsible
For having to educate you.'

John Foster

Good Morning

This is
the teacher forecast

Mrs Brown
will be gloomy with occasional outbreaks of rage,
storms are expected by mid-afternoon.

Miss Green
will be mild, although her smiles
will probably cloud over when she finds
the spider in her chalk box.

Mr White
will be rather windy, especially after dinner-time,
with poor visibility when his glasses fog over.

Some drizzle is expected around Miss Red,
she has not quite got over her cold,
and Mrs Blue is already gusting down the corridor
and should reach gale force 9 when she hits the
playground.

For the rest of you, it will be much as usual,
a mixture of sunny moments and sudden heavy
    showers.
Have a good day.

Dave Calder

Face the Front

It was a normal assembly.
Big kids at the back,
Little ones at the front,
Teachers at the side
And Mr Griffiths leaning against the vaulting horse.
Waiting.
Waiting for Class Four and Miss Phipps.
Again.

'Emma,' said Mr Griffiths,
'Go and tell Miss Phipps that
Assembly is about to begin.'
Off went Emma through the door at the back.
We all turned round
And watched the door.
Then Mr Griffiths said,
'Face the front.'
We faced the front.
Then the door banged.
So we all turned round.
It was Class Four. And Miss Phipps.
'Sorry we're late.'
'Thank you, Miss Phipps.'

'Michael,' said Mr Griffiths,
'Go and tell Emma that
We have found Class Four.'
Off went Michael through the door at the back.
We all turned round
And watched the door.
Then Mr Griffiths said,
'Face the front.'
We faced the front.
Then the door banged.
So we all turned round.
It was Emma.
'I can't find Class Four.'
'Thank you, Emma.'

'Now face the front.'
We faced the front.
Then the door banged.
We all turned round.
It was Michael.
'I can't find Emma.'
'Thank you, Michael.'

'Now will everybody face the front.
That includes you, Sarah.'
We all turned round to look at Sarah.
'There's no need to turn round. Face the front.'
We faced the front.
Mr Griffiths faced us.
Then the door banged.
We all turned round.
It was the wind.

Mr Griffiths shoved off from the vaulting horse.
He stamped to the back of the hall
And stood by the door.
'There! Satisfied?
You can all watch the door and me
At the same time.
Perhaps we can start the assembly.'

There was a mighty crash
From the front of the hall.
We all turned round.
Mr Griffiths' hymn book
Had slid off the vaulting horse.

John Coldwell

Why Are You Late for School?

I didn't get up
because I was tired
and I was too tired
because I went to bed late
and I went to bed late
because I had homework
and I had homework
because the teacher made me
and the teacher made me
because I didn't understand
and I didn't understand
because I wasn't listening
and I wasn't listening
because I was staring out of the window
and I was staring out of the window
because I saw a cloud.
I am late, sir,
because I saw a cloud.

Steve Turner

Excuses

Didn't have time, Miss
Had to go out.
Couldn't find my book, Miss
Please don't shout.
Mum forgot to iron my blouse, Miss
She said this one would do,
Yes, I know it's not a school one
Yes, I know it isn't blue.
Yes, I did my homework,
But Dad let the dog chew it,
I know you can't read it
But I really did do it.
I lost it on the way, Miss,
No, I don't know where.
I did have it on me.
Oh, it's just not fair!

John Cotton

Excuse Me?

My teacher is confusing me;
I wish she'd make up her mind.
Last week eighteen was six times three—
Today it's two times nine.

Aislinn and Larry O'Loughlin

Sum Haiku

All my sums are wrong
I wish I could go home now
Raindrops wash my face

Coral Rumble

Those Nine-Times Blues

Some teachers praise their pupils for turning up on
  time,
Some teachers give out golden stars for standing
  straight in line;
Some teachers smile in friendly style and some are
  just bad news,
But when I see that old Maths Man I get those Nine-
  Times Blues.

Well, it's: How many nines make forty-five?
            And nine into nine goes what?
            And if I divide thirty-six by nine
            How many nines have I got?
            Well if eighty-one is nine times nine,
            And there are seven in sixty-three,
            And then I call out a hundred and eight
            How many nines will that be?

Some kids are good at answers and their hands shoot
   up like trees,
Some kids keep getting golden stars, and pick up As
   and Bs;
Me, I'd like to shrivel and shrink and hide in my
   worn-out shoes,
So, whenever I see that old Maths Man I get those
   Nine-Times Blues.

Jack Ousbey

'And Then'

My teacher says
I mustn't say
'And then',
Like when I write,
'I went into the forest
And then I saw a huge bear
And then the huge bear
Lumbered towards me
And then I grabbed him
By the throat
And then . . .'

My teacher says
Every now
And then
I should stop.

But I don't know when.

And if I did
I might not get started again.

And then
I'd never finish the story.

June Crebbin

Writer's Worry

We're having a *'Book Week'* . . . !

Last time, it was 'Poetry'
And they made us *write* poems *each day*,
Which *was* hard enough—
But a *BOOK*! Well, *that's* TOUGH;
Now we'll *never* get out to Play!

Trevor Harvey

Spelling

The words
we've learned
are:

COULD
to rhyme with
SHOULD.
So far so
~~COULD.~~
GOOD.

WOULD
you explain why
RAIN
sounds the same as
REIGN?
I MEAN
as in
~~QUEAN.~~
QUEEN.

I am
FRAUGHT!
My temper is
~~SHAUGHT.~~
SHORT.

We ~~AUGHT~~
OUGHT
to complain.

Words
are
~~ABSORD~~
ABSURD.

Ann Bonner

Torture!

My palms are running
rivers of sweat
and my neck
starts to itch.

I shut my eyes
tight
lick my lips
pray
that my pencil
won't break
that I won't
forget.

Right,
says Miss Price.
Ready, class?
This week's
spelling test—
do your best!

Patricia Leighton

Wanted: A Magic Teacher

We want a *magic* teacher,
who clicks her thumbs—
ZAP!—we know sums:
who says a spell
so we can spell;
who waves a wand
and, instantly,
school stuff's so easy-peasy.
At 3.15,
just for a joke,
she'll disappear—in clouds of smoke.

Mike Johnson

As If By Magic

I don't like the way
things move about
secretly, when
you're not looking.

You can leave a pen
on your school desk,
turn to your friend
for a second, it's gone;

pencil sharpeners,
rubbers are the same,
always taking
magic holidays.

In the cloakroom
when no one's there
I think the coats and shoes
have a party,

play hide and seek,
dance with each other.
They rush back to the rack
when the bell sounds

but you can tell
what's been going on.
Nothing is ever in the place
where you left it.

Irene Rawnsley

My Teacher

My teacher once wore nappies
My teacher used to crawl
My teacher used to cry at night
My teacher used to bawl.

My teacher jibber jabbered
My teacher ran up stairs
My teacher wrote in squiggles
My teacher stood on chairs.

My teacher once was naughty
My teacher was so rude
My teacher used a bad word
My teacher spilled her food.

My teacher lost her homework
My teacher took too long
My teacher got detention
My teacher did things wrong.

My teacher's all grown-up now
My teacher can't recall
My teacher thinks she's different
My teacher's not at all.

Steve Turner

Wet Play

Rainy windows,
Rainy faces,
Peering out at
Rainy places.

In the classroom
On a tray
Games that no one
Wants to play.

Unkicked balls and
Unskipped ropes;
Unworn hats and
Gloves and coats.

Waiting for the
Wind to drop;
Waiting for the
Rain to stop.

Slowly it
Begins to clear.
Bright blue patches
Now appear.

Rainy clouds are
Blown away
And every one
Goes out to play.

Marcus Parry

Skipping Steps

Skipping in the playground
One-two-three.
Arms out, jumping high.
Hey, watch me!

Skipping at a double rate
Like boxers on the telly.
Wowee! Puff and pant,
Legs like jelly.

Taking turns at rope ends,
Laughing as we shout
Under-over-doublies,
Next one's out!

Harj faces Alison,
Two to a rope.
Billy tries to muscle in—
	SOME HOPE!

Time to fold the ropes up,
Time to get in line.
Can't wait for dinner time—
	The next turn's mine!

Patricia Leighton

Shoot the Messenger!

On playground duty, while sipping her tea,
Miss Martin told us stories.

'Long ago,' she said, 'if he brought bad news,
they used to shoot the messenger.

This bringer of bad tidings,
message hidden, horse hard-ridden,
would burst upon the scene
with news of some huge defeat
in battle.

And the first response would be,
pretend it hadn't happened,
make out they hadn't heard,
shoot the messenger,
forget his words.'

We listened, open-mouthed.
Miss Martin was smart,
her story must be true.

'Now,' she said, 'I've a job for someone.

Who wants to go to the staff room
to tell the teachers
it's end of break?'

Brian Moses

Show and Tell

A week last Thursday Mrs Bell
Said, perhaps for Show and Tell,
We could bring along some pets,
An idea that she now regrets.

There were cats and rats and dogs,
Miriam had brought some frogs,
Then shy and quiet Ursula
Took out her pet tarantula.

Children shouted, children shrieked.
Some stood on their desks and squeaked.
All of which just served to wake
Brian's favourite rattlesnake.

It shook its tail, as if to say
One shouldn't treat a snake that way,
Terrifying mice and rats
And Cathy's dozing vampire bats.

They rose as one into the air.
Amy leapt onto her chair,
Knocking over neighbour Grant's
Box of giant soldier ants.

Pets were crawling, croaking, creeping.
Mrs Bell just sat there, weeping,
When we heard a fearsome roar
And a head popped round the door.

In the room came Susie Bland
With a leash grasped in her hand.
'Quiet, boy! Now stay! Just wait!
It's my T-Rex. Are we too late?'

Paul Bright

I'm Special!

In our school
    I'm the only one
    who can zip around
    the playground
    at thirty miles an hour!
Watch out everyone. My
wheelchair is supercharged—
    I'm special!

In our school
    I'm the only one
    whose fingers know
    how you look, who
    never stumbles in the dark.
My eyes are in my fingertips,
my ears pick up every sound—
    I'm special!

In our school
    I'm the only one
    who can switch off
    our teacher's voice
    when I've had enough.
Sometimes I can listen in
to staffroom conversation—
    I'm special!

In our school
I'm the only one
who knows the names
of all the birds
along the riverbank.
I can't write them down,
but I can mimic every call—
I'm special!

In our school
I'm the only one
of me. No one else
thinks the same, speaks
or looks the same.
In all the world, I'm the only me.
Amazing, when you think of it—
I'm special!

Moira Andrew

Wasp!

That's not a fly—
it's yellow and black . . .
Wasp in the classroom!
Panic attack.

Squish it! Squash it!
Jump! Flap about!
Tip over tables!
Sit still! Teacher shouts.

Where has he gone?
We're tingling with fear.
Will he crawl up a leg
or buzz in an ear?

Yes! There he goes!
What an uproar.
Our panic's over—
He buzzed off next door!

Jane Clarke

To Get Off Games

Please, Miss, please, Miss,
I've very painful knees, Miss,
Please, Miss, please, Miss,
I think I'm going to sneeze, Miss,
Please, Miss, please, Miss,
I think I'm going to freeze, Miss,
Please, Miss, please, Miss,
Your lessons make me wheeze, Miss.

Julia Rawlinson

Changing Time

My favourite subject's Gym,
My worst is Changing.
It's a shame they go together,
That needs rearranging.

Frances Nagle

Two Onto One

Rachel's not friends with me.
She says that I smell.
She's poisoned Rebecca against me as well.
They won't share my hymn book,
Or help mix the paint.
They say if I'm near them
They both want to faint.
They're whispering about me
They giggle and lie,
I know tears will spill out
If I open my eyes.
Why are they mean to me?
What have I done?
It never seems fair
When it's two onto one.

Daphne Kitching

Billy Doesn't Like School Really

Billy doesn't like school really.
It's not because he can't do the work
but because some of the other kids
don't seem to like him that much.

They call him names
and make up jokes about his mum.

Everyone laughs . . . except Billy.
Everyone laughs . . . except Billy.

They all think it's OK
because it's only a laugh and a joke
and they don't really mean it anyway
but Billy doesn't know that.

Billy doesn't know that
and because of that
Billy doesn't like school really.

Paul Cookson

New School

The new boy sits alone
In the corner of the room.
He wonders will anyone be his friend.
He wonders when this long, long day
At this huge, huge school
Will ever end.
Will it ever, ever end?

John Kitching

School Time

We've got
a crooked clock in class.
Its seconds take
an hour to pass.
Except at playtimes!
Then it's bound
to be the other way around.

Jez Alborough

Packed Lunch

On the Sandwiches table
I sit next to Ronan.
He has jam in his
And I'd rather have jam
Than ham and lettuce
And he'd rather have them
So we change over.

And I give him my apple
Or nuts or grapes
In swap for his cake.

If Mum knew she'd hate it.
When she asks if I enjoyed my lunch
I don't lie. I tell her
It was much appreciated.

Frances Nagle

School Dinners

Adam takes a tiny bite,
Simon's fork and sausage fight,
Laura says she's leaving hers,
Alex sits and slowly stirs,
    Till the dinner lady says:

Hurry up and scrape your plate.
Hurry up or we'll be late.

Sarah's playing with her chips,
John's got ketchup on his lips,
Lisa's messing with her fork,
Anwar stops to have a talk,
    Till the dinner lady says:

Lisa, why's Anwar in tears?
Forks do NOT belong in ears!
Sarah! John! Now stop that game
—I'm pleased you've learnt to write your name—
But chips aren't pens and nor, I think,
Is ketchup meant as writing ink!

Celia Warren

Playing With Fire

Never cross our caretaker,
Never make him mad,
Never call him names
Or tell him that he's sad;
Never steal his tools,
Never nick his screws,
Never spike his coffee
While he's listening to the news;
Never laugh at his overalls
Even though they're baggy,
Never tell him that his tummy's
Getting rather saggy;
Never stay in the cloakroom
When he's trying to sweep,
Never make loud noises
When he's just gone off to sleep;
Never stuff your litter
Underneath his cupboard door,
Never drop your chewing gum
Upon his polished floor;
Never write your name upon
A desk with pen or pencil,
Never decorate his bucket,
Even with a stencil;
Never complain loudly
When his radio starts to boom,
'Cause he'll feed you to the dragon
He keeps in the boiler room!

Coral Rumble

Miss Jones, Football Teacher

Miss Jones,
  football teacher,
red shellsuit,
  flash boots.
She laughs
  as she dribbles,
shrieks 'GOAL!'
  when she
    shoots.

Miss Jones,
  what a creature,
pink lipstick,
  shin pads.
See there
  on the touchline
lines of
  drooling
    dads.

Miss Jones's,
  finest feature,
long blonde hair
  —it's neat!
She 'bend' kicks
  and back heels,
she's fast
  on her
    feet.

Miss Jones,
  football teacher,
told us,
  'Don't give up!'
She made us
  train harder,
and we
  won
    the cup!

Wes Magee

Christmas Play

We're doing the Nativity
And Sonia's being Mary
Jack's the Angel Gabriel
He's dressed up like a fairy.

I'm half of Mary's donkey
I made the tail in art
After last year I've been given
A non-speaking part.

James McFee is Joseph
And Ibrahim's a King
He's dropped his jar of frankincense
And Sonia's giggling.

1SB are shepherds
And they are still deciding
Who shall give the baby lamb
And who shall keep abiding.

Joseph asks the innkeeper
If they can stay the night,
'OK,' says Shaun, I push him hard
He never gets it right.

He hits my leg, I scream out loud,
The angels all stop praying,
Mary says to Joseph, 'Hark,
There's the donkey braying.'

The shepherds now have broken ranks
The Kings join in as well,
The stable rocks, the crib falls on
The Angel Gabriel.

'Away in a manger
No crib for a bed
The little Lord Jesus
Has landed on his head.'

* * *

Miss has got a cup of tea,
I give her my mince pie,
'Christmas comes but once a year,'
She murmurs with a sigh.

Petonelle Archer

Heads or Tails

I'm one half of a horse
in our school play
I really don't know
how it worked out this way.

I'd rather have been
an angel instead,
but at least we take turns
at being the head.

Andrew Collett

Best Day

'This is the best day of my life,'
said Jimmy to the school secretary.

'Oh, yes,' she said. 'Why's that?'
'I'm being sent home,' he said.
'Oh dear,' she said. 'Why's that?'

'Spots,' he said. 'All over.'

And he showed her.

June Crebbin

School Outing

Class Four, isn't this wonderful?
Gaze from your windows, do.
Aren't those beauteous mountains heavenly?
Just drink in that gorgeous view.

Sir, Linda Frost has fainted
Aw, Sir, I think she's dead
And Kenny Mound's throwing sandwiches round
I've got ketchup all over my head.

Oh, aren't these costumes just super?
Please notice the duchess's hat!
You can write up your notes for homework tonight,
I know you'll look forward to that.

Sir, Antoinette Toast says she's seen the ghost
Of that woman, Lady Jane Grey
And I don't know where Billy Beefcake is
But the armour is walking away.

And here in this ghastly dungeon
The prisoners were left to die
Oh, it's all just so terribly touching
I'm afraid I'm going to cry.

Sir, Stanley Slack has put Fred on the rack
Sir, somebody's pinched my coat
Sir, Melanie Moreland's dived off the wall and
Is doing the crawl round the moat.

Well, here we are, homeward bound again—
It's been a wonderful day
I know when you meet your parents and friends
You'll have so many things to say.

Sir, what is that siren wailing for?
Sir, what's that road block ahead?
Sir, Tommy Treat is under the seat
Wearing a crown on his head.

Gareth Owen

The Best Bit About a School Trip

I've been to the place
where the Vikings once lived
it must have been cold.

I've been to the farm, seen horses
rare pigs and multi-coloured sheep
it was very smelly.

I've been to the seaside
collected seaweed, paddled in rockpools
got my jeans soaking wet.

I've dressed up as a Saxon
a Roman soldier and a Tudor king
felt very important.

But the very best bit
is eating your sandwiches, swapping your crisps
for your mate's biscuits.

Swigging your pop
stuffing your face with your mum's best cake
and too much chocolate.

Piling into the shop
buying pencils, erasers and notebooks
spending your money.

I'm an expert at this
four years in Junior School
has taught me a lot.

David Harmer

Story Time

At the dark end of day,
Our work's put away,
And we all sit there
By the teacher's old chair
For story time.

Teacher reads in a whisper.
We don't say a word.
She reads about ghosts
And a magical bird.
She reads about silver
And jewels and gold.
She reads about witches
Wrinkled and old.
She reads about princes
In bright rainbow coats;
About troublesome trolls
And three trip-trap goats.
She reads about giants
And a weird magic bean,
Describing strange worlds
Which we've never seen.
She reads about poor boys
And princesses proud.
She makes us see camels
Hiding there in a cloud.
She's got hundreds of voices:
Gruff, gentle, shrill, deep.
Some listen with eyes closed,
But none fall asleep.
We all keep so still,
Not one word to say,
As we sit there quite hushed
At the dark end of day.

John Kitching

Down by the School Gate

There goes the bell
it's half past three
and down by the school gate
you will see . . .

. . . ten mums in coats, talking
nine babes in prams, squawking
eight dads their cars parking
seven dogs on leads barking

six toddlers all squabbling
five grans on bikes wobbling
four child-minders running
three bus drivers sunning

two teenagers dating
one lollipop man waiting . . .

The school is out,
it's half past three
and the first to the school gate
   . . . is me!

Wes Magee

Explaining to Gran

I told Gran about the Menu.
She told us what's for tea.
I told her, 'It's on the computer.'
She said, 'That's too hard for me.'
I told her I dragged with the mouse.
She said it sounded cruel.
It's pretty hard work telling Gran
what we do at school.

Jill Townsend

My School Report

Sitting in the bathroom
Troubled by the thought
Of Mum and Dad suspiciously
Sifting through my school report.

They've been reading for ten minutes now
And the silence makes me scared,
By the time they've read the *general* part
They'll surely want a *quiet* word.

I think they've finished reading now
They must be reeling from the shock,
So just for safety's sake I'll keep
The bathroom door on lock.

Ian Bland

A Sad Case

I've had a shock, my parents said—
That's why they've sent me up to bed.

My head still thumps!
My stomach aches!
I'm feeling faint—
I've got the shakes!
I can't believe
That it is true.
How cruel! HORRIFIC!
And—
My parents KNEW!

The teacher whom I LEAST adore
Has moved in—
TO THE HOUSE NEXT DOOR!

Trevor Harvey

Why Must We Go to School?

Why must we go to school, Dad?
Tell us, dear Daddy, do.
Give us your thoughts on this problem, please;
No one knows better than you.

To prepare for life, my darling child,
Or so it seems to me;
And stop you all from running wild—
Now, shut up and eat your tea!

Why must we go to school, Dad?
Settle the question, do.
Tell us, dear Daddy, as much as you can;
We're really relying on you.

To learn about fractions and Francis Drake,
I feel inclined to say,
And give your poor mother a bit of a break—
Now, push off and go out to play!

Why must we go to school, Daddy?
Tell us, dear desperate Dad.
One little hint, that's all we ask—
It's a puzzle that's driving us mad.

To find all the teachers something to do,
Or so I've heard it said,
And swot up the questions your kids'll ask you,
My darlings—now, buzz off to bed!

Allan Ahlberg